JOSEPH L. YOUNG

COURSE IN MAKING MOSAICS

an introduction to the art and craft

2

CONTENTS:

REINHOLD PUBLISHING CORPORATION
New York

Mural, Temple Emanuel, Beverly Hills, California, 1956,
by Joseph L. Young. Sidney Eisenshtat, A.I.A., Architect.

INTRODUCTION

 REPRODUCED THROUGH COURTESY OF PUNCH ALMANACK

Shades of Antioch

In ancient Greece, the city of Antioch had many pavements in marble mosaic depicting their deities. Recently, mosaic floors were designed for the main entrance to the National Gallery in London. Sir Winston Churchill, Edith Sitwell, and Bertrand Russell are represented in portraits that are witty satires on the Victorian virtues of "Wonder", "Curiosity" and "Open Mind". Currently, similar plans are afoot in Hollywood, California, where a community "beautification" program envisions mosaic portraits of film stars embedded in the sidewalks. The moral to this story: if the robed citizen of ancient Antioch could stroll upon mosaic representations of their gods, why should contemporary man be bashful?

Mosaics: America's 20th Century Folk Art

There seldom has been a word like mosaic (unless it is money), that means so many different things to so many people. Depending upon your personal taste and means, you can find a myriad of things described as mosaic; from a $5.95 "do it yourself mosaic kit" at your local department store to a fourteen thousand eight-hundred and fifty dollar bracelet advertised by Tiffany & Company of New York as a mosaic design.*

Just how Tiffany's elegant bracelet, "spirited with Near Eastern splendor", may have been inspired by the type of mosaic broach Cleopatra probably wore for Mark Anthony, is not all there is to be told. Like many things, it's the information between that's fascinating. Approximately 5000 years is as far back as the archeologists have been able to find examples of mosaic art. Of course, there are historians who suspect we may one day find mosaics much older, but there are many more people here in America who are more interested to find out why the revival of interest in Mosaics seems to have been born yesterday. Actually it wasn't!

4

5

Since Colonial times America has regarded the fascinating art of making mosaics somewhat the way a timid suitor courts a beautiful woman . . . mostly from afar. Nevertheless, affection grew, as can be seen by the oblique ways the word mosaic entered our language. It was first known either by its Old Testament origins as the Mosaic Law† handed down by Moses, or as pertaining to the ancient art of the Muses. From these Hebrew and Greek origins the word mosaic progressed to descriptive usages.

Farm experts employed the term to describe the virus condition of certain plant diseases; zoologists used the word to indicate the compound-eye characteristic of insects; and aerial topographers found mosaic a word ideally suited to explain the process of assembling terrain photos. But even such a fair daughter of European culture as mosaic, possessed of an ageless beauty sought by kings and empires, had to wait some time before a growing America could overcome its Puritan scepticism of permanence.

*"Of round sapphires alternated with groups of four diamonds in a platinum setting." The price as advertised included all federal tax.

†MOSAIC LAW — ancient law of Hebrews, moral and ceremonial, attributed to Moses; contained in Hexateuch, Pentateuch, and Joshua; also in Ezekiel XI-xlviii, as well as in Scriptures.

BEFORE GRANT TOOK RICHMOND! It took over a century before shy word usages warmed into a proper Victorian declaration of intentions. But today, we are immersed in a fantastic variety of things called mosaic; aluminum wall coverings, rugs, lampshades, store counters, wallpaper, record covers, cuff links, book jackets, mirror frames, shoe horns, coffee tables, shower stalls, and bottle openers. It now seems inevitable that a candy concoction labelled mosaic will be marketed.

This mass-production of facsimiles has obscured the fact that art performed the honors of introducing mosaic to America long before the Civil War. Perhaps one day the sociologists will explain it all; especially why any art only begins to have value to Americans if it reaches the sublime by first progressing through the ridiculous.

A MOSAIC IS A MOSAIC IS A MOSAIC: In early civilizations, the arts and crafts were an inseparable unit. In our time, however, we tend to think of mosaic in the categorical manner of a popular guessing game like "20 Questions"; i.e. anything made from vegetable (#5 Corn Palace, Mitchell, S.D.), mineral (#4 St. Mark's Cathedral, Venice, Italy), or animal (#8 card stunts at a University of Southern California football game), employs the technique and therefore is a mosaic.* Obviously, this kind of labelling can become endless.

Most of these conflicting meanings began during the Renaissance when the separation of Church and State divided the arts from their crafts. The Industrial Revolution widened the gap, inventing special names to identify newly mechanized crafts. But no new word was coined for the *craft* of mosaic and so, in our time, mosaic has come to mean the *craft* more often than the *art*. Even more frequently, the term mosaic is misused in such a way as to imply an adaption of the craft *is* the art. As heir to this divided concept, modern man is now rediscovering that mosaics have their greatest use and meaning (value and beauty) when the art and craft (form and function) are one.

Today, mosaics as a craft have found wide application as veneers for floors, ceilings, walls; as an art in integral-mosaics used to support structures; and as sculptural and transparent mediums. In all these methods, the final appearance of mosaic, either as works of art integrated within structures or as independent transportable panels, depends upon the needs of our architectural order. Since our industrial society is geometrically shaped in specific ways, the story of mosaic cannot be fully told without describing how our geometric or gridiron way of life in America formed our architectural order.

---

* The Encyclopedia Brittanica states: The making of mosaics is the art of assembling units of materials (stone, marble, metal, smalti, wood, ivory, etc.) and inlaying them into another material such as marble, stone, concrete, wood, ivory, etc. When the area of such inlays is larger than the exposed surface of the supporting materials (which thus becomes the base or support to hold the pieces of inlay) the result can be called mosaic.

THE MOSAIC OF EVERYTHING AND EVERYBODY: How often have you heard the expression, "Don't be a Square!", used to needle someone for excessive stiffness or overformal behavior? Odd as it may seem, this everyday phrase reflects America's growing interest in the arts. Like all folklore, it is a humorous rejection of all those ideas in the 20th Century that still insist all play as well as work can be based on pure geometric order; that same kind of order necessary to run our machine-tooled world where everything is prefabricated out of a grid plan. Anyone who has taken a plane trip across America has observed the vast geometric mosaic of our life unfolding; a heritage of checkerboard farms and gridiron-planned cities, passing below one like some monumental graph stretching into infinity. From cradle to grave, life is lived within this grid. It shapes how we develop the land, where we build, what we eat, when we sleep, and why we work.

Although sometimes this basic support can look and feel as menacing as an armored girdle, it is the foundation of our own making, to do with what we will. Recently, the overwhelming pressures of growth within the grid have forced alterations. To save our cities from strangling in their own traffic, new freeways (#10), are being built to go over, under, and right through the grid-planned city.

LONG BEFORE COLUMBUS DISCOVERED AMERICA: In Europe the radial city still prevails. Although tourists sometimes tend to regard the radial city as some sort of museum piece, it does let man live closer to nature. The art of mosaic grew up in this older agrarian or organic environment, starting with jewelry for royalty, and gradually progressing to a very developed art form. The Sumerians, Egyptians, Greeks, Romans, Early Christians, and citizens of Byzantium were familiar with mosaics done in everything from shells, metal, glass (#7), and wood, to marble (#12), stone, sand, and ivory. Nearly every conceivable scale, size, color, and shape of materials were tried at one time or another. The earliest mosaics were casual, decorative inventions based on organic shapes of nature. Slowly the art took on controlled, logical, and geometric forms as the first industrial methods grew out of the agrarian order of life familiar to the ancient world. The art of mosaic reached its Byzantine climax in the Cathedral of Haggia Sophia in Constantinople, a nearly perfect intermingling of East and West, with Christian philosophy acting as the catalyst.

THE TOTAL IMAGE OF BYZANTIUM: To those who have seen the splendor of Byzantine mosaics throughout Italy, it is not difficult to understand why this great era has captivated the contemporary mind. The organic unity of San Vitale in Ravenna for example, is the superb work of an anonymous master-mosaicist who worked in a way almost unknown to the extremely individual artists of our time.

8

9

10

11

Having but a single philosophy to express, the master-mosaicist's problems of content and form were preordained. Also, since it was customary that he be well paid for his efforts, his mind was free to tackle the problems of creation. This was his main job and he did it by telling the story of the Bible on the walls of the church. He began by translating his scale color study to the walls by painting (in a pointillistic manner that was to be rediscovered by Seurat, Pissarro and other French impressionists) with colors composed of raw pigment ground in lime-water. This rough fresco-type painting was done directly on the dried surface of the prepared setting bed (or scratch-coat of mortar).

The master-mosaicist's assistants, thoroughly trained to work as a team, then followed his bold color notation system (versus the outline system so often employed today) by first applying over the rough painting an additional coat of finer mortar made white with marble dust. This was done in patches from the top of the wall downward, and only as much as could be covered with tesserae within a half-hour, as the mortar set firm in that time. With a duplicate portion of the master's scale color-sketch in hand, and the master himself close by on the scaffolding to supervise, the assistant mosaicists selected colors with some degree of interpretation, and then pressed the stones directly into the cement.

Undoubtedly the master-mosaicist's supervision included holding the entire team of assistants within the over-all style, adjusting the light-reflecting angles of the stones to take advantage of the illumination, juxtaposing a contrasting color here and there to carry out the color vibration, and assuring consistency and quality of execution from day to day. Such an artist was truly a master of architectural scale. He, above all mosaicists who preceded and many who have followed, knew that the art of mosaic was more than an art of decoration.

EVERYBODY TALKS ABOUT THE WEATHER: Despite Mark Twain's famous remark, Byzantine mosaicists created materials able to do something about climatic conditions. In the Mediterranean countries, where heat and glaring sunlight are a problem, the builders of churches had to devise a means of keeping their large structures cool without shutting out all the light. It was solved by using smaller and often circular windows. This "funneling-in" of light through *bull's-eyes* was ideal for the use of glass mosaic; one of the few permanent materials flexible enough to express the purpose of the building while distributing the light.

Of course, the weather was just as important in the northern countries of Europe where the weak sunlight during the long winter made warmth and light desirable for the interiors of the large and drafty medieval cathedrals. Tapestries

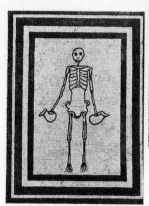

12

13

14

15

might be fine to lighten the gloom of a Hamlet living behind castle walls many feet thick, but the church as a sanctuary had less to fear, and could afford more light for the populace. It was the medieval artist who adapted the art of making mosaics to meet the problem of inadequate central heating. Instead of employing glass mosaics as a veneer with multiple functions, the opacity of mosaics was converted into the transparency of stained glass. Although temperatures inside the buildings only went up a few degrees, the Cathedrals looked warmer and attendance probably increased both in the North and in the South.

Despite all these practical accomplishments, the total image of the Byzantine and Medieval worlds crumbled with the rise of the Renaissance. Man turned back to ancient Rome and Greece for inspiration. Mosaics, so long in the service of the church, found itself without a patron. As all the arts became compartmentalized, mosaic was reduced to the survival level of a craft. Other than a few forlorn revivals, for hundreds of years the Goliath of art lay dormant.

HOW GILDED WAS OUR LILY? The use of mosaics in America, both as an art and craft, was very much influenced by immigration to the new world and the swift development of the tile industry. On the segregated level of fine arts, American architects before 1900 farmed out mosaic commissions to the workshops in Italy. It was an ornately imitative period and the artisans of Venice flourished, scaling the drawings and pasting the mosaic on paper to be shipped back to the United States for installation in prefabricated sections. The end result often revealed that architect and artisan were more than oceans apart, that is unless the architect undertook the role of an artist also and went to Venice to supervise the commission. Even then the crated mosaics sometimes got wet during the return voyage and arrived an indecipherable batch of mosaic swimming in dough-paste.

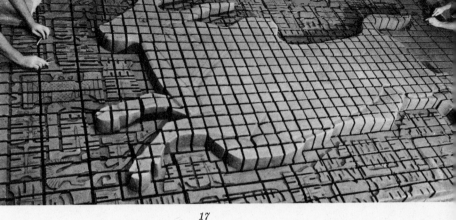

16

17

TOM SWIFT AND HIS MECHANICAL MOSAIC-MAKER! After 1900 the emigre tile and mosaic workers tried to adjust to the new industrial world of America by adapting their hand procedures to the swifter techniques of building. Setting mosaic by hand was quickly abandoned in favor of the man who operated a simple metal grid (#15) and could set many square feet per day. Soon after, the man was replaced by the machine (#16), and the change from the organic way of working to the geometric was complete. Since the art of mosaic was never suited to the manufacture of facsimiles from prototypes, the grid system substitute that was offered to replace mosaic had to be a mechanical checkerboard image

As a result, before World War I, the term mosaic began to be used to describe tile work. Most of the workers in mosaic found they could make a better living installing terrazzo or tile imitations of mosaic; Greek floors for banks, Byzantine motifs for Turkish baths, and Roman fretwork for railway terminals. From concert hall foyers to hotel bathrooms the antiseptic white of thousands of tile installations moved through the growing cities of America like a giant glacier. Machine-made imitations of mosaic became so inexpensive they wound up gracing tenement house entrances.

The Industrial Revolution taught us to cover millions of square feet of flooring cheaply; however, the price included almost a quarter of a century without the rich color, texture, and art within authentic mosaic that helps make life more enjoyable. On the other side of the ledger must be recorded two important facts, both of which have indirectly benefited the art of mosaic. Just as the painter recognized the futility of competing with the camera, the mechanization of the tile industry has obviated competition between the mosaicists and the machine. Also, we must not forget that in many respects our tile industry is unsurpassed in the world today and, because of this accomplishment, has provided a fine new source of durable and inexpensive materials for the mosaicist.

The second period of mosaics in America coincided with the raccoon-coated prosperity of the 1920's. Architects and artists of that generation completed their education in Europe. When this avant-garde returned, the berets were put away, and among the architectural souvenirs brought back was a classical respect for mosaics.

Mosaics, instead of being restricted to flooring, were elevated to something one looked at. Framed wall areas in buildings were reserved for murals, and muralists were commissioned to design mosaics. As disciples of Blashfield, Brangwyn, or Parrish, they worked in the prevailing mode of their day. This meant being a facile manipulator of oil paints; anything more was not considered necessary since the 19th century academies of art had established the dictum that the execution of mosaics, true-fresco, and stained glass were crafts, and as such they were mediums a true maestro designed for, rather than worked with.

However, the sending off of mosaic designs for execution in Italy sometimes became too costly in terms of time, and so mosaic studios were started in America. Since most of the successful architects in the 1930's-1940's were very involved in the impossible task of recreating a dead past, the American mosaic workshops were seldom sought out to produce original works. The quality of artisanship in some shops excelled because they were supervised by artists who had taken the time to study in Europe and master the principles of creatively executing from their own designs. Too often the general quality of work seldom went beyond making skillful mosaics out of what should have remained uninspired paintings. The hopeful side to the American scene came with the end of World War II.

ART AS A BY-PRODUCT OF THE MACHINE! While the art of mosaic was living in a state of suspended animation in America on the fine arts level, it was being prepared for a metamorphosis on another and more important level; a rebirth via the unforeseen by-products of our mass-production system. The "division-of-labor" concept that nearly destroyed mosaic as an art, became the progenitor of a widespread and basic revival. As we have seen, until World War II the technical knowledge required to make mosaics had been relegated to a craft limited to a handful of mosaic workshops and tile contractors.

The revival of mosaics in Mexico, and 25 years of accumulated technological advances in America changed the scene overnight; less expensive pressed-glass mosaics were put on the world market as Italy's answer to America's keenly competitive tile industry; improvements in adhesives seemed to pour out of the laboratories, better cutting tools and supports were developed; more knowledge became available on mounting papers, colored grouts, and water-soluble glues.

After lying dormant for almost 400 years, the art of mosaic has begun to awaken throughout the world, returning as one of the most important integrating arts of the 20th century. In Mexico, Italy, France, Switzerland, Germany, and in America the accomplishments have taken on dimension and scope. Perhaps the 20th century has come full circle in history to pick up the values that were discarded by the Renaissance. Perhaps mankind has recognized the need of the symphonic light and color in mosaic to build a new total image. Perhaps the art once made by slaves for kings, and once used by the Church for the people, now will become one of the true arts of the people?

If this hopeful vista lies ahead, it is because of the increased leisure time which shorter working hours produced. During the depression few people imagined so many people would ever have the free time to discover there is more to recreation than sports, travel, and TV. Also, how few ever dreamed we would find ourselves a nation of skilled specialists forced to find our way back to hand arts we abandoned because we cannot afford to hire our counterparts? These are some of the forces that brought forth the "do-it-yourself" movement in America and what better example than mosaic kits?

HOW FAR CAN PROGRESS PROGRESS? Almost anybody can do a creditable mosaic, if a reasonable amount of time is devoted to learning the craft. The colors are so bright and clean, one can also be easily misled into doing badly conceived and executed mosaics. Mosaic kits have both of these possibilities, i.e., while none can honestly claim they will teach you to do a masterpiece, many do offer the convenience of assembled materials and tools. Anything that encourages people to become genuinely involved in the creative experiences of art is a healthy thing; one must make certain it is actually art and not a facsimile being passed off as art. When it comes to mosaic kits, the danger of a facsimile begins when the manufacturer is not content to offer tools and materials, but throws in instructions and sets of designs to copy. It would be wonderful if these were *creative* in approach, but, more often than not, they are mediocre, trite designs pretending to teach through technique alone.

No one can measure the harm done by encouraging people to believe they can create art by buying a kit that distorts the fundamentals of the craft; i.e., because this approach generally starts the beginner with copying someone else's designs. It has nothing to offer the beginner interested in developing his own creativity. It is most important to examine the merits of a kit by first looking at the quality of tools and materials provided. Then check which authority in the field of professional mosaicists did the manufacturer employ to design and assemble the kit. More concretely, Gino Severini, the great French mosaicist (see page 55), summed up this point when he said, "Ancient mosaics have aroused much interest and admiration because of the perfect union of art and craft. In the work of today unfortunately, this accord is often missing. It cannot possibly exist if the art is done by one person and craft by another." If the future of automation in the United States will give enough people more time to trust the artist in themselves, then progress will progress pretty far.

STATUS QUO VADIS: Alongside this growing enthusiasm to participate in the arts are many architectural artists throughout the world who deserve the attention of every student of mosaic. Antonio Gaudi, the great Spanish architect, whose integration of mosaic and form in La Sagra Familia Cathedral in Barcelona, is admired by sculptors and mosaicists as well as architects. Thousands of visitors to Rome have discovered Pietro and Annamaria Cascella's magnificent mosaic mural in the railway terminal. Unfortunately, it is also true that most of the professional world of art and architecture is manacled by a *status quo vadis* concept and lives by the premise that all art is not one. The creative uses of mosaic has always been dependent upon the existence of an imaginative architectural order, an order that fulfills all human needs by employing the directional character of great artists.

In Southern California's famed Los Angeles, it is many miles between the oil rigs covering the Baldwin Hills, Lloyd Wright's Wayfarer's Chapel on Portuguese Bend, and Simon Radilla's strange mosaic towers in Watts (#20). And yet all these seemingly unrelated works are very important to the future of mosaic; especially if viewed as the legitimate grandchildren of Paxton's Crystal Palace in London of a century ago, or the Galleria in Milan, the Eiffel Tower in Paris, and the Brooklyn Bridge in New York. Throughout these remarkable structures the advantages of lighter and stronger supporting members were used. The structural wall was eliminated, or glass substituted, and imaginative engineering opened up possibilities for the future.

However, this left only the beams, glass, floors and ceilings as workable surfaces for the artist, unless the building was completely enclosed to be serviced by electricity and airconditioning. While engineers like Buckminster Fuller of the United States, Pier Luigi Nervi of Italy, and Felix Candella of Mexico have been furthering a more organic approach to architecture, the artistic potential of the "open" structure was first sensed by a self-educated artist named Simon Radilla. For 25 years Simon Radilla covered the supporting members of his fantastic, 100 foot towers with mosaic made from the discarded crockery and bottles found on junk-heaps.

Recently Nicholas Schoeffer, without having seen the Radilla Towers, used sound in addition to color and form in his "spatio-dynamic" tower for a park in Paris. In the field of transparent screen-walls for buildings, many artists have been at work.* And where the enclosed structure is paramount, the opaque modular-mosaics in stone by Mexico's Juan O'Gorman demonstrates the ability of an artist to dominate

*Jan de Swart, Emile Norman, Robert Mallory, Sam Kaner, Ray Rice, Roger Darricarrere, etc.

18

21

19

20

22

the grid system and make it support a functional expression. Now that some of the extremes of opacity and transparency have been explored, most likely a synthesis of these elements will formulate the new direction in the art of making mosaics.

The general public, and particularly the professional world of art, must look to the creative architectural artists of our time if the gridiron system is to be used as a means to expression. Today, the gridiron system often appears to be the end aspiration in the arts. However, as the means and ends are harmonized, all these specialized and segregated concepts within the world of art will be absorbed into a total image of our society. If our time is to face this challenge, our artists will have to expand the meaning and purpose of art until it can provide science with the kind of goals that will integrate the diverse directions of man.

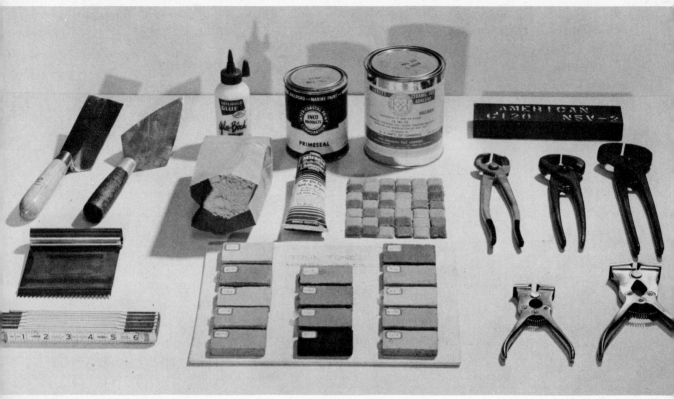

23

(#23) For spreading adhesives
(left) spatula, trowel, notched
spreader; adhesives (top, center) Wilhold glue, sealer, a can
and a tube of ceramic tile adhesive; abrasive stone to file fine
cuts of mosaic, and under this,
five types of carbiloid-tipped tile
cutters; (center) grouting cement, samples of ¾-inch square
mosaic glass and mineral oxide
colors for coloring the grout.

Tools & Materials

The first requirement is a work area with
good light, a sturdy table, and adequate storage
space for tools and materials. Select an area
that is not accessible to children or pets, and
where the flooring can be covered readily with
a protective layer of cardboard. A simple shelf
arrangement with transparent plastic containers or glass jars is practical for storing colors.
An assortment of bowls for mixing grout is
necessary, as well as a small garbage can to
store magnesite or cement. If you do not wear
eyeglasses, inexpensive plastic goggles afford
protection when cutting glass, tile, or stone.
Tweezers are handy for placing fine cuts, and
a screwdriver is useful to remove mistakes after the mastic has dried. Nail polish remover is
excellent for removing dried adhesive from the
fingers, if you are not allergic.

Pressed Glass or Vitreous Tesserae. This is the
least expensive of the Venetian or Mexican
glass mosaics. It comes under various brand
names (Muranite, Padovan, Pelv, Sarim, Sar-
ma, Saivo, Talia, Vetrital, Vetrum, Mosaico Ve-
netiano etc.) which are basically similar in that
they are machine-produced in 15 to 100 colors
and cost between $1.65 to $6.00 per square foot,
depending on colors. They come in ¾-inch
squares, 225 pieces mounted on 1-foot square
sheets of paper, approximately ¼-inch thick
with beveled edges to facilitate installation.
Before purchasing any quantity of pressed
glass mosaics, it is important to know none of
them equal the quality of Byzantine glass
(smalti tipo antico). Upon comparison, pressed
glass appears grainy in molecular structure and
the colors pastel in appearance. The grades of
quality within the pressed glass brand names
can be determined by test-cutting several tes-

Many craftsmen use natural rocks, pebbles, and semi-precious stones for making mosaics. In addition to the wide range of natural rock and stones available to residents at the beach, in the desert, or in the country, urbanites can find as many as 16 natural colors of crushed rock or gravel by surveying local building supply dealers. Colored rock or gravel comes in various sizes, ranging from pea-sized gravel called Standard Crush, to 1-inch and 2-inch Crush. Colored rock or gravel is packaged in 100-pound sacks, and one sack will cover approximately 24 square feet about ½-inch thick. (#24)

24

Fulget marble pebbles (#25) containers of Byzantine glass mosaic tesserae; (lower left) examples of Lake Como marble mosaic tiles (a prefabricated veneer) and a sample of ¾-inch square mosaic mounted on paper. All of these materials are from Italy.

25

The variety in composition of antique colored glasses suggest that the earliest forms of glassmaking grew out of metallurgy and/or out of firing ceramics. Byzantine glass is made up of sand and various combinations of soda, potash, or lead depending upon the particular color and type of glass desired. Since Byzantine glass is an inorganic material, with a minimum coefficient of expansion, it is ideal for all types of architectural uses. (#26) Sand and alloys used to make Byzantine glass being melted in furnace in Venice. Temperatures range from 2500°F. upwards. (#27) Molten glass being poured on to framed slab from clay crucible. (#28) Cutting glass tesserae by hand.

26

serae: the thinner glass mosaic is more difficult to cut accurately. To overcome this tendency to crumble or fracture in unpredictable directions, the cheaper glass has to be scored with a glass cutter before using the tile nippers. *Byzantine Glass Mosaic or Smalti Tipo Antico*. This finest of all glass mosaics is available in a wider variety of sizes, but the most common is ½ x⅜-inch face and approximately 5/16-inch deep, rectangular in form, with irregular edges. This hand-made material comes in a range of 5,000 hues and is preferred by professional mosaicists. The material, manufactured in Europe, is imported in bulk lots retailing on the average of $5.00 per pound (equals $15.00 per square foot) depending upon color, quality, and quantity. *Ceramic Tiles and Marble Tesserae*. There are numerous firms in the United States who manufacture various lines of ceramic tile, glazed and unglazed, suitable for mosaics. These tiles (as well as those imported from Italy, Spain, Puerto Rico, Mexico, etc.) are the least expensive, approximately $1.00 per square foot and often ideal for the beginner. Marble or

Marme tesserae (cubes), manufactured in Italy, are among the most expensive materials used to make mosaics. Casavan-Carrara Marble Co., Inc., 1 Mount Vernon Street, Ridgefield Park, N. J. is one of the principle importers of the material. *Selection of adhesives*, is determined by the type of mosaic you are making. Where a utilitarian mosaic is going to be exposed to moisture, as in out-door swimming pools or patios, it is customary to embed these mosaics in a mortar made from cement mixed with sand and water. For interior mosaics, ceramic tile adhesive, or magnesite, are recommended. When purchasing ceramic tile adhesive, look for the circular hallmark seal on the label which guarantees the ingredients comply with the U. S. Department of Commerce Standards. Sure-Bond, Miracle 3M (MMM), Armstrong, Chapco etc., start at $2.00 a quart (enough to cover about 10 square feet). Tile adhesives are also suitable for smaller mosaics meant to be in contact with water if you select an adhesive manufactured to resist the alkaline of mortar, and a water-proof grout is employed. Among

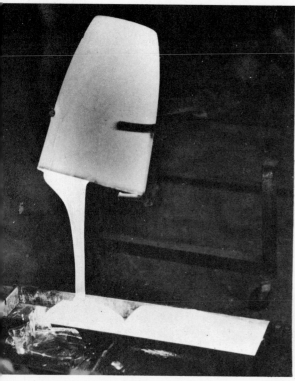

27   28

the names to look for here are Pioneer Latex, Crossfield Products, Armstrong, etc. To further insure the tesserae will not fall out after installation, prime the surfaces of particularly smooth glass with Armstrong J1190. *Supports* for mosaic panels can be made from Novoply or 5-ply Marine plywood. Novoply is an ideal base upon which to make a transportable mosaic panel or table. It can be bought in 4-foot sheets, either 8, 10, or 12 feet long and cut to the required dimensions. Professional mosaicists reinforce this support with a welded iron frame designed to prevent warping, but this need not concern the amateur unless he is tackling a mosaic over six square feet. *Glass or Tile Cutters*, pincer type with carbiloid-tipped blades come in several well-known brands (approximately $6.00) such as Superior Channelock, Red-Devil, Goldblatt etc. The Starett Company in Atholl, Massachusetts manufacture an adjustable jaw, double-leverage design that is especially useful for fine·cutting; in all instances the carbiloid-tipped blades are recommended, since they will outwear untipped

nippers. If the nippers become dull after prolonged use, take them to a tool maker or return to the manufacturer. Carbiloid tips must *not* be ground, but heated and drawn for sharpness.

Sources of Materials and Tools

CALIFORNIA, *Los Angeles:* M. Flax Art Supplies, 10846 Lindbrook Drive, West Los Angeles; M. Large, Box 45764; Los Angeles Tile Jobbers, 3371 Glendale Blvd.; Terry Tile Co., 5200 West Washington Blvd.; U. S. Tile Co., 8864 South Main St. Joseph L. Young Mosaic Workshop & School, 8426 Melrose Ave. *San Francisco:* The Dillon Tile Supply Co., 252 12th St.; Western Mfg. Co., 149 Ninth St. *Hollywood:* The Mosaic Tile Co., 829 N. Highland Ave. FLORIDA, *Miami:* Eastern Tile & Marble Co. ILLINOIS, *Chicago:* International Crafts Inc., 325 W. Huron St. MASSACHUSETTS, *Boston:* Hatfield Color Shop, 161-3 Dartmouth St. NEW JERSEY, *Summit:* Cermicraft, 6 Morris Turnpike. NEW YORK, *Long Island City:* Candon & Son. *New York City:* Agency Tile Supply Co., 336 E. 33rd St.; Bon Bazar, 228 W. 4th St.; The Door Stores, 247 E. 51st St.; Palazzo Trading Co., 931 Second Ave.; Leo Popper & Sons, 143-6 Franklin St.; Scharff Trading Corp., 414 E. 75th St.; The Workbench, 46 Greenwich Ave. Other organizations that have been active in the field of mosaic: Larry Argiro's Mosaic Workshop in New Paltz, New York, and Positano Art Workshop, 238 East 23rd St., New York City. OHIO, *Cleveland:* Immerman & Son, 1020 Euclid Ave.; The Potter's Wheel, 11447 Euclid Ave. *Zanesville:* The Mosaic Tile Co.

Direct Method

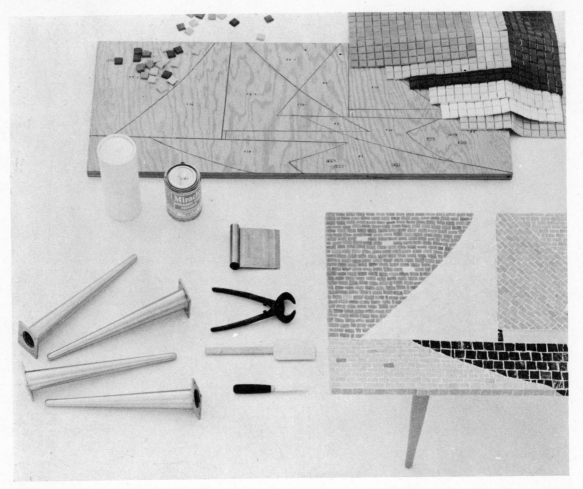

29

It is wise to gain preliminary experience by making a small trivet in mosaic, or by covering an unglazed ashtray with mosaic. Here, the main principle to master is the application of each tessera directly, one by one, either by pushing them into an area of mastic put on the surface with a spreader, or by buttering each piece seperately, and then applying it. In making a mosaic table in the *direct method,* first attach the legs to the panel to provide a working height, then size the top surface of the plywood with a sealer applied with a paint brush. After this dries, pencil in the outline of your design in a simple manner that allows for variety of color and directional placing of the tesserae. While these processes are being carried out, the one-foot square sheets of ¾-inch mosaic should be soaking in a pail of water to facilitate removal of the paper. Next, the paper should be peeled off from the mosaic and the tesserae carefully washed with warm water to remove any excess glue. The mosaic should be thoroughly dried with rags before applying

them, otherwise the ceramic adhesive will not stick effectively. Notice that the tesserae have a face, or front side which is smooth, and a back side which is beveled along the edges.

If a colored grout is preferred, mineral oxide colors are available at most tile outlets and should be thoroughly dry-mixed with the grout before mixing with water. Final cleaning can be done with steel wool and rags. If the table is for outdoors, or will be washed frequently, use a waterproof grout. Since the project generally takes the beginner approximately 30 to 40 working hours, the lid of the adhesive should be firmly shut when not in use, otherwise the adhesive will dry out. As an added precaution, a protective film of water can be put in the can before closing. Dump out *all* water *before* the mastic is used, as any water remaining will affect the adhesive. To those who want a functionally level table, a carpenter's level is a useful tool. However, the indirect method of installation is recommended if this is the quality you desire to have.

Basic tools and materials required to make a coffee table: approximately seven one-foot square sheets of ¾-inch square glass mosaic mounted on paper; a panel of 5-ply Plywood for a base; container of grout; small can of Miracle Ceramic Tile Cement; set of legs; metal spreader to apply adhesive; tile clippers; and two sizes of spatulas, a large one for the grouting process, and a small one for buttering adhesive onto tesserae. Note the way to hold the tessera backside up for buttering (#30) and how the spatula is used to apply adhesive. Starting with a corner is the best procedure (#31). Work down one side of the table by spreading the mastic out in advance with the larger metal spreader, and place the tesserae with approximately 1/16-inch spacing between, (#32). Gauging how to cut, an unbuttered tessera is placed over the intersecting line on the design, and the angle to cut marked in pencil. Cutting should be done face side up with the tile cutters biting into rather than across the piece. After completing the table, fill the crevices between the tesserae with cement (a process called grouting). Mix the grout by slowly adding water to the cement until it has the consistency of loose cake batter. The grout is worked quickly into the crevices with the rubber spatula (#35) and the excess wiped off with a damp sponge or cloth. Grout has a tendency to dry fast and so work should progress quickly.

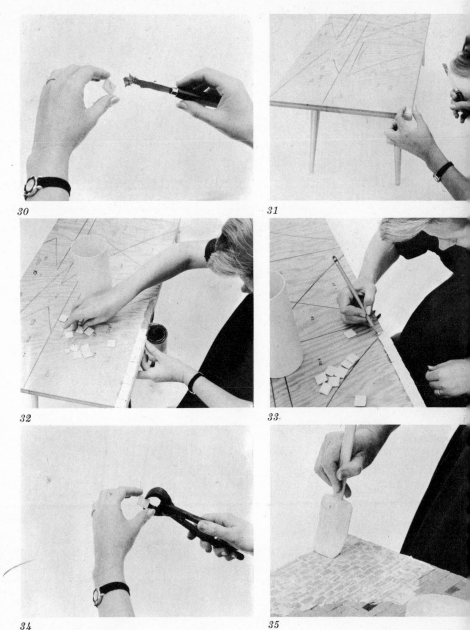

30

31

32

33

34

35

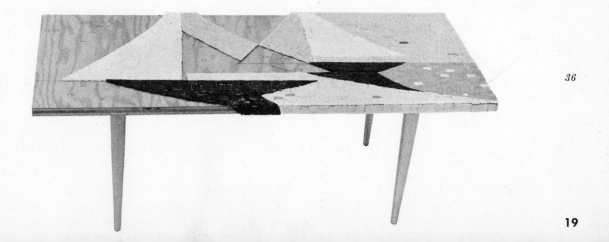

36

Indirect Method

37

The paperback or *indirect method* of making mosaics is most commonly practiced where a flat and functional surface is desired. Here, a round table was designed and executed by Sylvia Rosenthal for her Palm Springs, California home with the guidance of George Millar, Los Angeles mosaicist. The use of a balanced geometric design, based on the face of a compass, eliminated the necessity of executing the mosaic design in reverse.

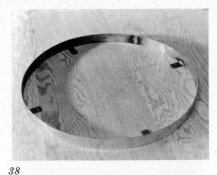

38

39

40

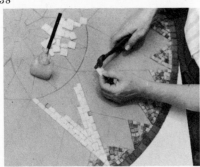

41

42

Circular brass frame (1¾-inch wide) was used as guide to cut plywood frame which then screwed into frame and legs attached (#38). Surface of setting bed inside frame was painted with one coat of sealer (#39). Following scale design, the tesserae are pasted with rubber cement to heavy paper, which was patterned and cut along the inside dimensions of the frame (#40). Cutting with carbiloid-tipped tile cutters (#41), each piece was carefully fitted to the next until design was completed (#42). Magnesium chloride was mixed with Magnesite powder (#43) in a plastic container with a wood spoon to make a lightweight cement (for interior use only). When mixture reached the consistency of wet mortar (#44), it was used to fill the setting bed until the magnesite could be leveled by pulling a board across the surface (#45). The completed mosaic was lifted, turned over, placed into position on the magnesite (#46), and firmly leveled out by hand (#47). After the mosaic had set for five hours, Bestine was applied with a rag to dissolve the rubber cement (#48), and paper pulled away (#49). Surface was grouted and polished with rags to complete the table.

43

44

45

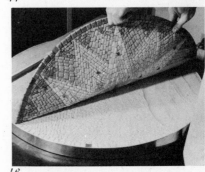

46

47

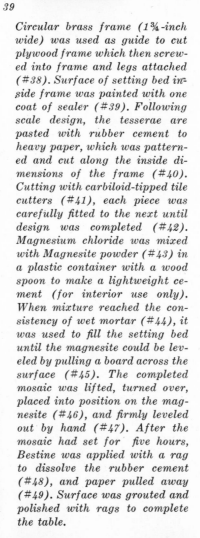

48

49

Suggestions on Cutting

50

(#50) Mosaicist Larry Argiro of New York, is shown using a pair of carbiloid tile clippers to fracture glass mosaic. Maximum leverage is gained with relaxed gripping of tool toward the end of its arm. This is less tiring and establishes a consistent way to measure how much pressure is required for each particular cut.

All cutting is based on variations of the square or circle. In order to plan the cutting of a mosaic, the beginner should experiment within these basic shapes. For example, half a square is two equal rectangles; divide one of these rectangles in half, and two smaller equal squares result. A diagonal line across a square will make two triangles. This also suggests subdivisions that are useful to study. The main value of this approach is that it offers a systematic way to explore the scope and scale of sizes most satisfactory for each particular project.

How well this approach works depends on how the cutting tools are manipulated. Fundamentally, there are two ways to cut mosaic: with a mosaic hammer and chisel, or with tile clippers. Both methods are based on a fracturing process. The older system of using a hammer is still preferred by many professionals; however, since custom-made hammers are not available on the American market, the beginner should use a tile cutter.

Familiarity with what the tile clippers can and cannot do comes from practice integrated with study of how the mosaic masterpieces of the past were cut. Techniques of cutting are based on the particular fracturing characteristics of the materials employed. For example, the cutting of many types of marbles, stones, rocks, and pebbles require power tools that saw, tumble, or grind rather than fracture. Therefore, it is advisable to use these materials either in their natural state or in precut sizes.

Byzantine glass, because of its finer molecular structure, fractures differently than the thinner and less opaque ¾-inch squares of mass-produced mosaic. Each color in all grades or qualities of mosaic has a different fracturing characteristic or "cutting feel," and these too, should be memorized. Ceramic tile tesserae are easily cut with the spring-type tile clippers, and, generally, are of more even cutting consistency from color to color.

Clean, crisp, and accurate cuts also depend

on how the tessera is held between the cutting blades. The tessera should be held by the thumb and forefinger at a 90° angle to the cutting blades, otherwise the glass will crumble or fracture inaccurately. Normal wastage for beginners learning to cut sometimes runs as high as 50%, but with practice 20% should be maximum. In all instances the scraps should be saved for future work.

When cutting a Byzantine glass tessera into equal parts, exact cuts can be achieved by placing the entire piece between the blades; the ¾-inch glass mosaic squares fracture more accurately if approximately ¼ to ½ of the tessera is inserted between the blades. Do not hold the tile clippers too close to your face while cutting, as flying glass can be dangerous.

It saves time when working on large areas to precut groups of shapes and sizes in advance, and to be sure an adequate range of color is available. Much of the final tactile and optical beauty of a mosaic depends on the self-discipline employed while cutting. In a well-cut mosaic every tessera has its precise place, and the total result gives the impression that all the tesserae are permanently locked into an organic unity. It is when this caliber of cutting skill is combined with a creative use of color perspective that the power of expression in mosaic becomes effective.

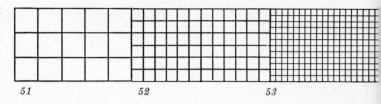

51   52   53

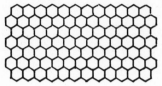

54

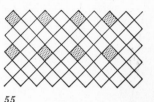

55

56

Five examples of ways to cut mosaic: glass mosaic tesserae used primarily in square and rectangular shapes (#57); ceramic tile cut in such a way that triangular tesserae appear to dominate the composition (#58); stones and pebbles used in their natural state (#59); rectangular shaped tesserae assembled in a calligraphic or baroque manner (#60); and an example where the cutting was subordinated completely to the use of larger grout areas (#61).

57   58   59   60   61

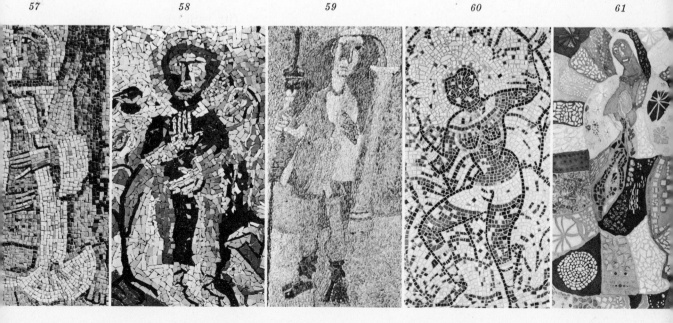

Doing a Wall Panel

Many beginners starting a wall panel try to emulate painting, an approach that unfortunately resembles neither painting nor mosaic. One practical way to avoid this pitfall is to study the making of mosaics as an art, an art that developed its own particular craft because it can do what other art forms cannot. Mosaic is an architectural art form where a bold and creative use of the tools and materials is essential. Here, George Millar, well-known California mosaicist, demonstrates how he designs and executes a wall panel in the direct method. The design, in this case, stressed an interpenetra-

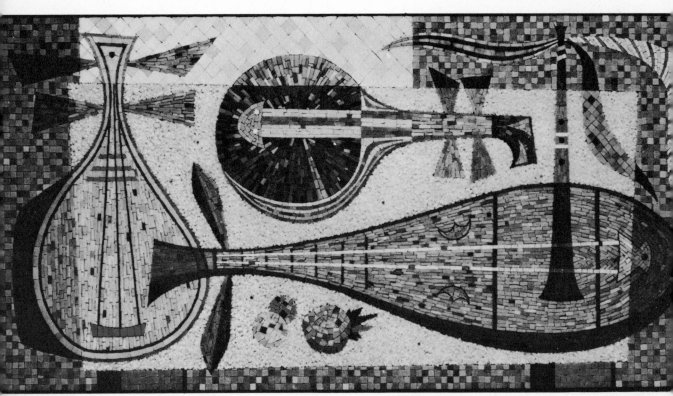

62

tion of shapes where the color, values, and planes are integrated. The final accents of the musical instruments were achieved by highlighting the strings with specially selected brass strips. Such a panel is not beyond the abilities of many beginners if emphasis is placed on a creative approach. Mosaic is an art medium that takes time to execute. To retain a spontaneous expression is always a problem. The technique of execution requires a coordination of manual skill, patience, and knowledge, three disciplines that should always be excited by the challenge of creative ideas.

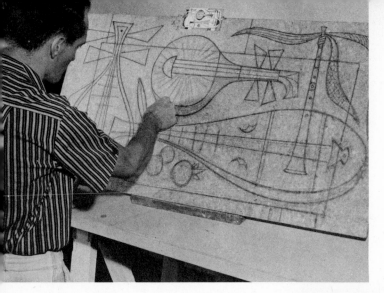

(#63) Working from a scaled sketch, mosaicist George Millar prefers to outline the forms in charcoal so that he can rework the shape relationships while planning how he will lay the mosaic.

63

(#64) Great care, patience and skill are devoted to cutting; to use the tool efficiently, the tile clippers are held with the head of the nippers facing the hand holding the tesserae. The tile clippers can be operated equally well left handed or right-handed.

64

65

(#65) Wilhold Glue is applied in a small dab to the specific place on the design where the tesserae is to be placed. The tesserae are placed face upward and exactly where they are wanted. Since the glue is quite strong when it dries, corrections are difficult to make afterwards.

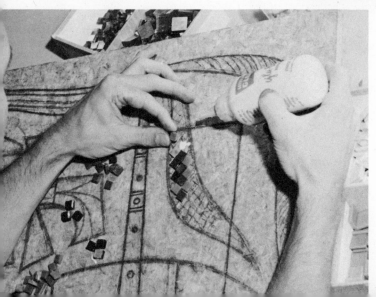

66

These photographs illustrate the type of advanced project which interests beginners who have completed a wall panel and understand the fundamentals of designing a mosaic for execution. Here, mosaicist Ray Rice of Sausilito, California is shown creating a *utilitarian* mosaic table, and an *integrated* mosaic over a fireplace for the Braun and Heller residences in San Francisco. In both cases, the indirect method of first pasting the tesserae down on paper was employed. Note how the artist subdivided the paper-mounted mosaic into sections to facilitate installation. On smaller projects of this nature, it is possible for the artist to do the installation; however, on larger mosaic murals it is advisable to employ the professional skills of union tile setters familiar with installing mosaics. Also note that the artist started the installation at the base of the fireplace and worked upward. This is standard procedure in America; in Europe mosaics are installed by starting at the top and working down. Each system has its advantages. The American technique prevents the mosaic units from sliding down the wall; an event that sometimes occurs when installing a mosaic mural during a very wet day. The European system saves time on larger projects as it requires only one wash-up of the installed mosaic after the paper is removed; a most important advantage when the mosaic is so large that it requires more than one day to install.

68

67

Projects for Home and Family

(#70) For those who prefer a rugged outdoor feeling in their living room, this iron and mosaic fireplace, designed and executed by David Tolerton and Louisa Jenkins of Big Sur, California, is a fine example of effective collaboration between sculptor and mosaicist.

(#71) Rock and glass mosaic mural designed and executed for the dining room of Joseph Mitchell's home in Los Angeles by Kayla Selzer.

(#72) Mosaic and plaster bas-relief mural designed and executed by Hugh Wiley for the foyer of the Perrin home in New York City.

70

71

72

73

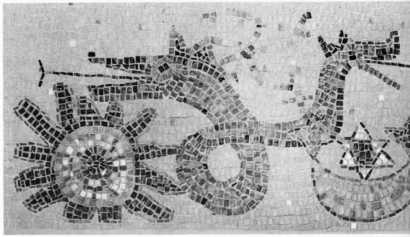

74

75

(#73) Here is an interesting example of what can be done with a door-knob; designed and executed by Kayla Selzer of Los Angeles.

(#74) Fritz Faiss, noted artist of Northridge, California, demonstrates his well-known versatility in this "Seamonster" mosaic fantasy for the swimming pool of the Helwig home; this was executed in a variety of Byzantine mosaic colors, including gold leaf tesserae.

(#75) An example of mosaic tile flooring manufactured by the Capoferri brothers of Bergamo, Italy. This material, reminiscent of ancient Greek floors, has found wide use as patio flooring both in America and Europe, and goes under the name of Fulget. Here the stones are embedded in a cement form and the tiles produced can be arranged into many designs.

(#76) Garden planters can take on a handsome durability when covered with mosaic, as exemplified by this imaginative installation done in ¾-inch square mosaic for the Bantam Cock Restaurant entrance in Los Angeles.

(#77) Byzantine mosaic has found application also in contemporary lamp bases as designed by Nicholas and Larry Argiro of New York. Here smalti, ¾-inch glass mosaic, and brass were combined.

76

77

79

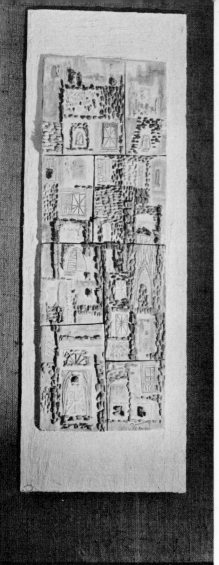

78

(#78) An original combination of materials was worked out in this "City Scene" by ceramicist Lois Stearns, by super-imposing Italian-made smalti on hand-made clay tesserae.

(#79) Mosaics done in marble have a subtle appeal that is sometimes deceptive. Although they often are done in a simple, direct manner, the design and execution requires the full abilities of a top professional. This "Unicorn", done by Joseph Lasker, demonstrates that a fine mosaic requires more than craft to become a work of art.

80

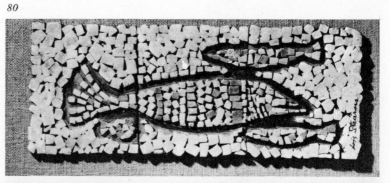

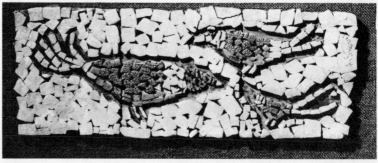

(#80) In both the "Lobster" and "The Birds", Lois Stearns moulded clay into units that were glazed and fired; a technique that can be traced as far back as the Sumerians, nearly 5,000 years ago.

81

82

The sharing of esthetic experiences does not have to be vicarious, especially with the possibilities offered through the medium of mosaic. Making a mosaic as a family, or group project, can offer great satisfaction to participants of all ages. On the left above, artist Emmy Lou Packard is shown assisting two of the 560 children from kindergarten to the sixth grade who participated in making a 126 square foot mosaic mural for the Hillcrest Elementary School in San Francisco. They worked in shifts of six children and completed the work in 27 days. Beach pebbles, broken ceramic, stained glass, abalone shell, and glass mosaic were applied in the direct method with 3-M ceramic tile adhe-

isve (CTA-11) onto seven panels of ¾-inch exterior grade plywood (which were later bolted to the wall).

The Werts family of Los Angeles, worked on a rectangular mosaic mural titled "The Queenship of Mary Most Holy" for their home. Commercial unglazed tile manufactured by The Mosaic Tile Company of Zanesville, Ohio, was applied with Wilhold Glue to a surface of reinforced ¼-inch masonite. The Werts project was carried out under the supervision of the Adult Education Program of the Immaculate Heart College directed by Sister Magdalen Mary, I.H.M. On both projects cutting of tesserae was minimal and no grout was employed.

83

84

85

(#85) Basic reference books and drawing materials used by professional mosaicists. A reducing glass is useful to evaluate color combinations. Spade-shaped brushes and square pastel sticks are ideal tools for doing a cartoon.

Doing a Cartoon

The making of a full-scale cartoon, to be executed in either the direct or indirect method, is an essential procedure for the beginner to master. It is here that the coordination between juxtaposition of colors and cutting of the tesserae is planned. Only the most experienced professional mosaicists have enough knowledge to successfully create a mosaic without first doing a cartoon. In the past, cartoons for mosaic murals were first done on paper in gouache, or watercolor, and an outline tracing of the design made to transfer either onto a special paper for mounting the tesserae, or onto the wall prepared for installation. This was preceded by a thorough scale study in color in which the mosaicist strictly adhered to using only those colors available in the mosaics at hand. However, since most contemporary artists generally do not embed their work into cement with a grout, unless making a utilitarian surface, it becomes a great time saver when making a wall

panel to draw directly on the supporting board with square sticks of pastel colors and/or with a square-nibbed mechanical marking pen. The same is true of large mosaics to be done in the indirect method. Better results can be obtained by most beginners if the outline concept is avoided, as the filling in between outlines tends to produce a mechanical-looking image. Here, time can be saved by doing the cartoon in color directly on the paper to which the tesserae will be mounted; middle-toned papers are best suited for this purpose. A plastic spray fixative will prevent the pastels from smudging. It is best to work boldly on the general concept and then develop details. But most important, think in terms of mosaic as you draw; instead of using the sweeping continuous movements more common to drawing and painting, the pastels or marking pen should be manipulated with the fingers so that the same sweep is expressed in a series of short, staccato-like strokes that swell

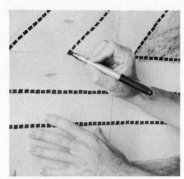

86

87

88

89

(#89) A full-scale mosaic cartoon done in pastel on double-
ply, non-shrinking, toned paper.
Tesserae were mounted directly
on paper after cartoon was cut
up for prefabrication. Note the
one-inch equals one-foot scale
study on the right; and how the
full-scale cartoon on the left was

drawn in reverse for the final
installation; the cartoon is always done backwards in the indirect method, so that when the
completed prefabricated sections
are turned over into the cement
during installation, the final
mural is identical to the first
sketch. This mosaic mural of

Byzantine glass was designed
and executed for Don Bosco
Technical High School, South
San Gabriel, California, by Joseph L. Young, 1956. Barker and
Ott, AIA, Architects. Installation by Premier Tile & Marble
Company. (See photo #141 for
the completed mosaic mural.)

and diminish in size, thereby indicating each
tessera quickly and clearly as to shape, color,
and its relationship to its neighboring tessera.
The square-shaped pastels are ideal for this
purpose since they are relatively inexpensive
and match the approximate width of the most
commonly used Byzantine glass tesserae. Also,
the pastel color scale as shown in #89 is more

than adequate to indicate most over-all color
combinations, if it is assumed an elaboration
of color will take place during the final selection
and cutting of tesserae for mounting. On this
page is a series of suggested drawing exercises
which can be used as a guide for those beginners
interested in developing their own way to do
a cartoon.

Executing and Installing a Mural

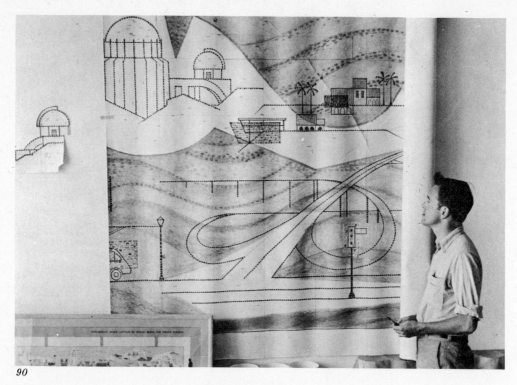

90

The author commenced design of this 6 x 36-foot cantilevered mosaic mural by number-ing sections and planning how to cut them up as the drawing of the cartoon progressed.

91

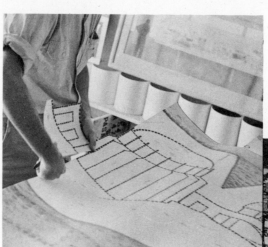

92

(#91) *After expanding the 1-inch equals 1-foot scale color study into a full-scale cartoon on heavy double-ply paper, the en-tire cartoon was cut into pre-determined units one foot square each for the mounting of the tes-serae on the paper. Non-shrink-ing paper was used to assure accuracy of the final dimensions.*

(#92) *Stone by stone the Byzan-tine tesserae were laid out in a preliminary mock-up directly on the sectionalized cartoon to co-ordinate color, seaming, cutting, and scale.*

93

94

95

96

97

The tesserae were fractured with a mosaic hammer and chisel (#93) and then mounted on the paper (#94, 95, 96), illustrating the indirect method of execution. The completed detail (#97) is ready for checking against the cartoon before stacking and storage.

98

99

(#98) The mural was reassembled on the floor at the site of installation for a final check. Here the author is shown making final adjustments of the seams.

(#99) After the author, and head tile setter Ira Cooper, reviewed the blueprint procedure for installation, the units of the prefabricated mosaic were picked up from the floor and placed on a tile-setters work bench, where each unit was buttered with ¼-inch layer of colored grouting cement.

100

101

102

A similar coat of cement (#100) was evenly troweled onto the cantilevered panel in preparation for the prefabricated one-foot square units (#101). Each piece was tamped into the cement with a hammer and block (#102), and checked to see if it was level with its neighbor. Notice that the installation occurred from bottom to top.

103

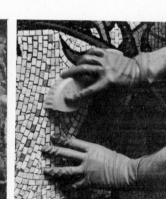
104

Once all the units were in position, the cement was allowed to set for forty-five minutes before the paper was moistened with water, and removed (#103). The surface was then cleaned by scrubbing with water to remove remnants of glue and excess grout. Several days later the mural was given a final muriatic acid scrub-down (#104 — six parts water to one part acid — use with extreme caution), and polished with dry rags.

105

Mosaic mural for main lobby of Los Angeles Police Facilities Building, designed and executed by Joseph L. Young; Welton Becket FAIA, & Associates, Architects; installed by Premier Tile & Marble Company and AFL Tile Setters Local No. 18 of Los Angeles.

The Mosaic Technique in Other Media

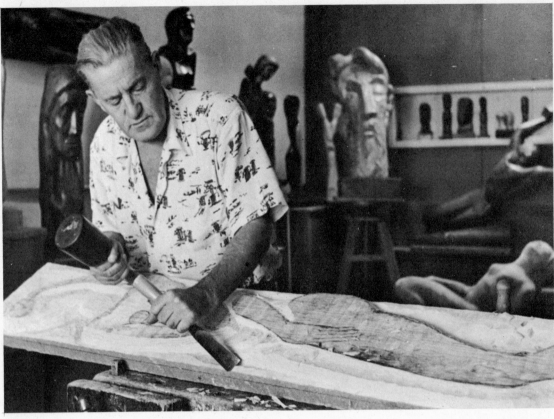

106

After the main forms of the bas-relief were carved (#106), a ¾-inch deep setting bed for the mosaic was routed out of the wood, and the Byzantine tesserae cemented into position with Ceramic Tile adhesive (#107). Next, the untinted grouting cement was mixed in a plastic container and swiftly brushed into the crevices between the stones (#108), and the excess wiped off with a sponge. The final step of staining the wood to bring out the grain (#109) also acts as a preservative for the wood while darkening the color of the grout. Completed panel is opposite.

107

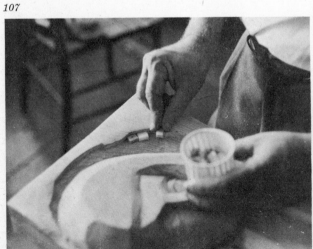

108

WOOD—MOSAIC—SCULPTURE
by Charles Schlein

As a wood sculptor, I became intrigued with the idea of incorporating wood and mosaic. My first and most difficult problem was to bring together what seemed to be two unfriendly mediums. In order to work toward plastic harmony and avoid unnecessary complications, I started with a design vertical in form and content. The carving was done directly while keeping in mind the union of mosaic to follow. As I carved, I stopped periodically to place the tesserae along the outline of the figure to formulate the background: the moment I placed the crisp glass mosaic against the softer grain of the wood, the wood seemed to lose its personality. Despite the various color harmonies I tried, the mosaic dominated the sculpture. It became obvious that, in this type of bas-relief, the placement of mosaic tesserae flat on the surface emphasized the aggressive character of the glass and set up a conflict with the more docile wood. After much experimentation, I tried recessing the mosaic by carving channels, or setting beds, around the figure. This was the answer. It enabled me to place the tesserae flush with the background surface of the wood, thus equalizing wood and glass. To contrast the wood surface with the lighter-toned mosaic, I dissolved shoe polish in turpentine and brushed it onto the surface, quickly wiping off the excess with a clean rag. The grain of the wood appeared strong, and the mosaic took the role necessary to this particular union. A great deal of experimentation will have to be done in this field before all the exciting possibilities will be understood and applied.

109

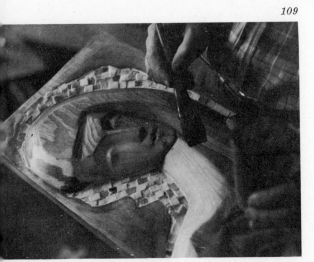

110

111
"Grasshopper" by Eugenie Gershoy of San Francisco.

SCULPTURE, MOSAICS AND COLOR

Many people have wondered why the ancient world combined color and form with such ease, while today, the majority of sculptors prefer either monochromatic forms or geometric constructions in primary colors. Other than recent experimental exceptions*, from the Renaissance period on down, sculptors have avoided color. The *mosaic-technique* of assembling works of art is no different today than in the past, and yet most sculptors in our time select materials and develop forms that preclude the use of color.

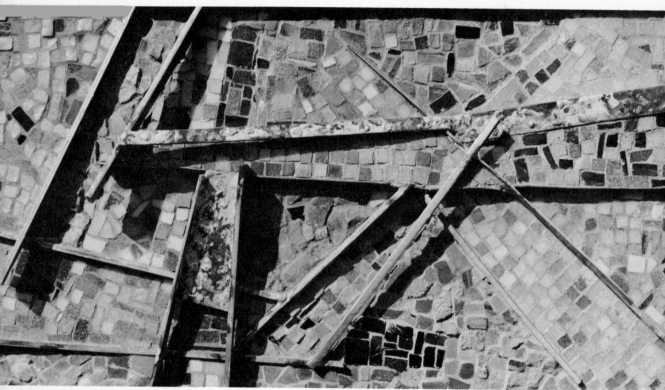

112

"3-D Abstraction", bas-relief mosaic in pressed glass, ceramic tile, potsherds, and brass, by sculptor Ted Egri of Taos, New Mexico.

An important re-evaluation of the past has occurred during the last few years and is initiating a return to basic concepts. Sahl Swarz, well-known American sculptor, recently said: "Our own time is notable for its lack of chromatics in sculpture, mainly due to the difficulty in achieving an integrated feeling between color and form. But in mosaics, the glass pieces are the form itself, instead of a superficial embel-

*Max Bill, Alexander Calder, Pietro Cascella, Gyorgy Kepes, Gabe Kohn, Fernand Leger, Egon Moeller-Nielson, Moholy-Nagy, Irene Rice Pereira, Pablo Picasso, Ray Rice, Diego Rivera, Nicolas Schoeffer, Sahl Swarz, Antonio Tomasa, Elbert Weinberg, Ossip Zadkin, Steve Zakian.

113

"Tattooed Man", a three-dimensional mosaic sculpture built up with magnesite superimposed over an armature of pipe and wire, by mosaicist Ray Rice of San Francisco.

#114 "Menorah", Temple Emanuel, Beverly Hills, by Bernard Rosenthal, Sidney Eisenshtat, AIA, Architect. #115 Bas-relief concrete mosaic mural, Olivetti Showroom, New York City, by Constantino Nivola; Peressuti, Belgioioso & Rogers, Architects.

115

116

lishment. The surface, due to the hand cutting of the glass, is alive; it vibrates with diverse reflections at all angles. Color areas can be naturally modified for complementary relationships by mixing the colors to take advantage of the pointillistic effect of the medium. In other words, the colors are not solid; they are made up of endless fragments with cement between, so that their spacing and prominence can also be varied. This adds up to an unusual opportunity for pleasing manipulation."†

Architects, sculptors, artists, and designers are becoming concerned with a reintegration of all the arts in our time, and mosaic (as one of the most complete organic methods of using color ever developed by man) has already earned the right to lead the way.

†From article in January, 1955 issue of American Artist entitled "Sahl Swarz makes a new approach to an ancient art."

#116 "Crucifix", stained glass and welded iron, by Ted Egri of Taos, New Mexico. #117 "Bird Fable", sculptured ceramic tile mosaic by Irene Berchtenbreiter of Los Angeles. #118 "Madonna with Birds", sculptured ceramic mosaic by Jean Buckley of Los Angeles.

117

118

TRANSPARENT MOSAICS
Stained Glass

Artists of today are re-examining the ancient roots of their art, and the fascinating relationship between stained glass and mosaic. As a direct descendent of mosaic, stained glass became one of the world's most magnificent arts; so completely fulfilled that it has tended to repeat itself for hundreds of years. However, the strength of this traditional outlook has not deterred contemporary architectural artists from pioneering in the creative uses of colored glass. No longer is stained glass bound by the medieval laws that dictated a window must be constructed with leading and rods. Today, there are artists, Roger Darricarrere, Peter Ostundi, Robert Mallary, Sam Kaner, Jeanne Reynal, Don Charles Norris, Emile Norman, and many others, who are employing the mosaic technique to find new structural means to create transparent and translucent planes that will fill the needs of contemporary architecture.

The photos on this page show how a professional artist-craftsman, Roger Darricarrere, uses the mosaic technique to assemble his structural stained-glass windows in concrete. The chunks of colored glass, made by the artist with equipment of his own design, are 1 to 3 inches thick, capable of remarkable prismatic effect when chipped by hammer (#119). Instead of employing traditional leading, Darricarrere embeds the glass in steel-reinforced, concrete joints from ¼-inch to 10-inches wide according to the design desired (#120). Highlights are obtained by varying the thickness of the glass and cement.

123

Robert Mallary fractures the stained glass with a hammer to obtain fortuitous patterns (#121) which are then laid, often in many layers, onto a transparent sheet of plexiglas, resting on a special glass-topped worktable lighted from below. In order to control the frosting of the plastic, various transparent powdered materials were sifted onto the surface (#122), before and after the plastic was poured (#123). The plastic, which can be colored and/or textured before it is poured, locks the pieces of fractured glass together by seeping through the layers to the plexiglas base.

122

121

In the field of experimental mediums, Robert Mallary's work is well known and admired. Mallary collaborated with artist Dale Owen during 1955 to create a 6x37 foot translucent mosaic mural made of stained glass and plastic for the Escoffier Room of the new Beverly Hilton Hotel in Beverly Hills.

The use of both sharp and blurred edges is one of the special features of Mallary's technique, which relates it to painting as well as stained glass and mosaic. In describing his own work, Mallary recently wrote: "Luminous color and light, and what might be called *light-textures* offer great possibilities, and I often think of my work as simply an extension of stained glass and mosaic. While I do think that technical experimentation alone is not enough justification for a work of art, I do believe that the excitement of research can lead to good art. Indeed, the value of a new medium can only be demonstrated by the quality of the work which emerges from it."

"The Seven Days of the Week", a 6 x 37-foot translucent mosaic mural made of stained glass and *plastic, designed and executed by Robert Mallary and Dale Owens in 1954-55 for the Beverly Hilton* *Hotel, Beverly Hills, California. Welton Becket FAIA & Associates, Architects.*

124

125

126

Plastics

In addition to the work being done in bonding and laminating plastics, artist Sam Kaner of New York has discovered that the thinner ¾-inch square pressed-glass mosaics have a limited range of color with translucent characteristics (#125). Kaner has done many unusual and successful projects by mounting mosaic on sheets of plexiglas with a special transparent adhesive, and illuminating these panels from behind.

In quite a different direction Bill Hammon of Omaha, Nebraska, and his wife Nadene, collaborated with Leonard Thiessen to make their own opaque tesserae by hand-forming a soft plastic called Pyracon which hardens when fired in an ordinary kitchen oven at 350°. Above in the "Penitents", (#126), the desired colors were first mixed by pushing and squeezing the different colors available and then embedding these onto a layer of unfired Pyracon. Both sections were refired at the same temperature so that they fused into a single unit.

#127 COLORED SAND

From the molecular use of silicates, the next step-up in tesserae size is sand. Here is an example of the work of Leonora Cetone of Los Angeles, who adheres colored sands to masonite with Wilhold glue to make sand mosaics.

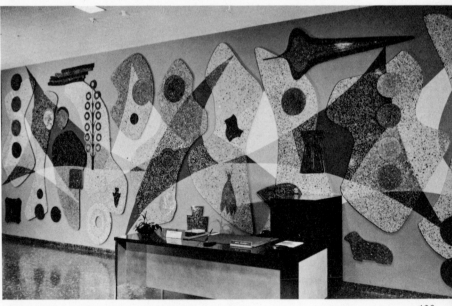

#128 TERRAZZO MOSAICS

Few American families have been more active in the field of mosaics than the Bruton sisters of California. All three have done mosaics in rock and glass. Here is an example of Margaret's work in terrazzo for the Standard Federal Savings & Loan Association of Los Angeles; Welton Becket FAIA & Associates, Architects.

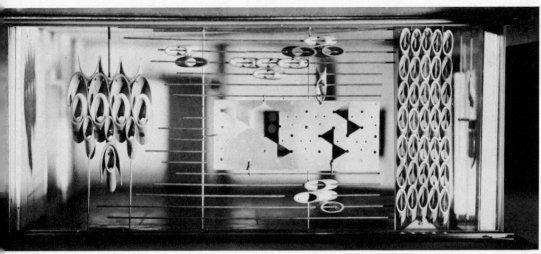

129

130

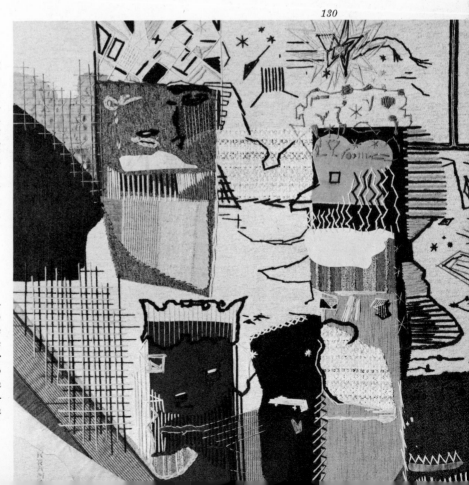

#129 METALLIC SCREENS

The potentialities of metal
sheets, rods, and extruded shapes
assembled in a mosaic-technique
is being explored by many artists today. Muralist Robert Lep-
per of the Carnegie Institute of
Technology, Pittsburgh, carried
out this particular project in
conjunction with Alcoa. Notable
work in this field is also being
done by Harry Bertoia (#9),
and Mary Callery of New York.

#130 THREAD MOSAICS

Today, the art of making tapestries is no longer restricted to
the loom, as exemplified by this
imaginative thread mosaic "The
Nativity", by Albert J. Kramer
of Los Angeles. Other artists who
are doing outstanding work in
this field include Everett K. Stur-
geon of New York, and John
Smith of Los Angeles.

EXAMPLES OF MOSAIC MURALS

PUBLIC BUILDINGS

Marble mosaic mural, side entrance to La Rinascente Department Store, Milan, Italy, designed by Massimo Campigli; executed by Giovanetti of Rome; Carlo Pagano, Architect, 1950.

131

Ceramic tile mosaic mural, Pershing Municipal Auditorium, Lincoln, Nebraska, designed by Leonard Thiessen and Bill J. Hammon in collaboration with Harry J. Macke, Art Director of Cambridge Tile Company, Cincinnati, Ohio, who carried out prefabrication. Architects: Davis, Wilson, Craig, Hazen, Robinson, Schaumberg & Freeman, 1957.

132

133

Italian glass mosaic mural, 17 x 51 feet, main lobby AFL-CIO Building, Washington, D.C., designed by Lumen Martin Winter, NSMP, executed by BMPIU No. 2 members with Ravenna Mosaic Company, St. Louis, Missouri, 1956.

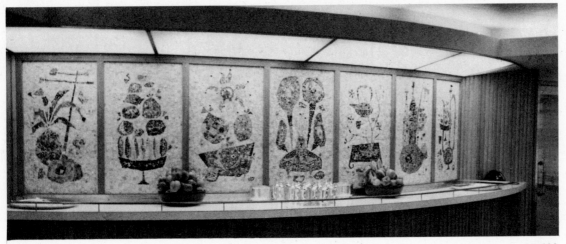

134

Seven mosaic panels for main dining room of S.S. President Coolidge, American President Lines, designed and executed by John Smith, 1956.

135

1,200 square foot Byzantine glass mosaic mural, lobby of 711 Third Avenue, New York, designed by Hans Hofmann, executed by V. Foscato, William Lescaze, Architect, 1956.

"*Symbols of Ancient Commerce*",
*marble mosaic for Commerce
Building, Madison, Wisconsin,
by James Watrous, 1957.*   136

*Mosaic mural in plaster, Cald-
erone Theatre, Hempstead, Long
Island, New York, designed by
Max Spivak; executed by V. Foscato; William Lescaze, Architect.*   137

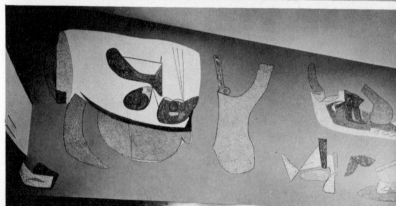

*Unglazed ceramic tile mosaic
designed by Ada Korsakaite,
Leighton's, Fifth Avenue, New
York; Victor Gruen and Associates, AIA, Architects, 1956.*

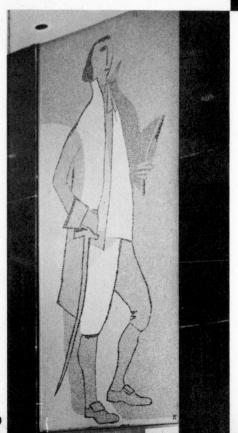

138

139

Marble mosaic mural, exterior entrance to Wasson's Recreation Center, Winnipeg, Canada, designed by George Swinton; Charles Faurer, Architect, 1956.

Glass mosaic mural integrated into rock screen of lava, Canlis Broiler Restaurant, Hawaii, designed by Ben Norris; executed by Bumpei Akaji; Wimberly & Cook, AIA, Architects, 1956.

140

Byzantine glass mosaic mural, 9 x 16 feet, main entrance to Don Bosco Technical High School, South San Gabriel, California, designed and executed by Joseph L. Young; Barker & Ott, AIA, Architects, 1956.

141

142

"Lux et Veritas", ¾-inch square glass mosaic mural, 4 x 29 feet, High School, Hudson Falls, New York, designed and executed by Larry Argiro; Sargent, Webster, Cranshaw & Folley, AIA, Architects, 1955.

52

143

Detail of tile mosaic murals, El Centro Escolar Idependencia, Morelia, Mexico, designed, executed, and installed by Robert Hansen, 1953.

144

"Greek Chorus" mosaic mural, Penthouse Theatre, University of Washington, Seattle, Washington, designed and executed by Jean Beall, 1955.

145

Italian glass mosaic mural, Allen-Bradley Building, Milwaukee, Wisconsin, designed by Edmund Lewandowski; executed in Venice, Italy, 1957.

146

147

Two panels from a "Stations of the Cross" series designed and executed in mosaic by Louisa Jenkins of Big Sur, California for the Mt. Angel Abbey in Oregon, 1953.

The "Star of David" and the "Menorah", two symbolic panels for a Jewish Temple, designed and executed by Ada Korsakaite in unglazed ceramic tile.

148

TWO OUTSTANDING
MOSAICISTS

149

Without question, one of the most significant mosaicists in our time is Gino Severini, now living in Paris. If his only accomplishment rested upon creating the link between the color theories of Impressionism and the form concepts developed by the Cubists, this alone would be a record of a brilliant career. However, Gino Severini went on to demonstrate that the future of modern art depends entirely upon the artists willing to meet the architectural needs of our time.

Gino Severini

While in Rome in 1901, Gino Severini met Boccioni, who was later to become the leader of Futurism. In 1906 he moved to Paris and worked alongside Braque, Picasso, Dufy, Utrillo, Valadon, and poets Max Jacob and Apollinaire. During this period his paintings were inspired by Seurat. As one of the signers of the Futurist manifesto, he arranged the meeting between the Futurists and the Cubists, and went on to fulfill his early promise by painting "Pan-Pan at the Monico", the acknowledged masterpiece of Futurism. After the Cubists saw Severini's paintings on exhibition in the first Futurist exhibition held at the Bernheim-Jeune Gallery in 1910, many of the Cubists abandoned their monochromatic approach to return to color.

True to his early Italian influence, Severini gravitated toward the direction being developed by Leger, Metzinger, and Gleizes. This concern with the monumental found expression in a series of frescoes executed for the Montegufoni Castle near Florence, in 1922. In the many productive years that followed, he painted frescoes and executed mosaics for churches in Semsales, La Roche, Fribourg, and Lausanne. In addition, Severini executed many notable mosaics in Italy and France for public buildings, and is highly

55

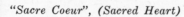
"Sacre Coeur", (Sacred Heart)

regarded as one of the rare artists who spent his life insisting upon the essential sense of permanency that must return to art.

Gino Severini, as the major international leader in the art of mosaic today, has written a magnificent volume of memoirs, and has lectured on the art of mosaic throughout Europe. The following quotes, translated by Beulah Roth of Los Angeles, are excerpts from his correspondence with the author, and from his address, "Mosaics and the Art of Murals in Ancient and Modern Times", which he delivered at a conference in Ravenna, Italy in June 1952, under the auspices of The Society for the Friends of Art.

"In each form of expression, but especially in mosaics, design and technique are *inseparable*. Technique reveals what is deepest in man; the eternal need to create something with his hands. A need which is a will, a hunger. In the mosaicist's hands everything takes life, from the hammers and chisels to the stones and enamels. They become vibrant and impatient as a ballet dancer waiting to go on stage."

"It is necessary for there to be an accord between painting and architecture. It implies not only a conception of space but a clear understanding of chromatic values so as not to destroy with color what was constructed with line. If I have so much interest, and I might add so much love, for that marvelous form of art, Mosaics, it is because I have so much respect for the materials which characterize it. Mosaic can be a powerful force in reintroducing order, clarity and purity into Art. It can also bring to Art a sense of reality which the modern world with its antagonists can no longer do."

"Basically, the artist does not want to be understood. Often, he suffers most from being understood. What he most desires is to last through the ages. The mosaicist is surrounded by an atmosphere of contradiction, and like all other artists he has to live in it and work in it. I believe that even the exigencies of a mosaicist's career should by no means prevent him from participating in the hope of other artists. Such associations will help him to choose the direction which suits him best and help protect him from the seduction of extremist thought."

150

151

Detail from mosaic mural, Church of St. Pierre, Fribourg, Switzerland.

152

Juan O'Gorman

MOSAICS — MEXICO — O'GORMAN
by Esther McCoy

It is not by chance that the integration of mosaics into architecture in our time was first achieved on a monumental scale in Mexico. Juan O'Gorman's library at University City, in which an acre of exterior walls are entirely covered with Mexico's history visualized in millions of stones, gathered from many states of the Republic, occurred not only by the happy coincidence of O'Gorman's combined gifts as muralist and architect, but is the result of Mexico's traditional love of completed buildings. Throughout its history, Mexico has used its walls for the expression of artistic feelings, making art inseparable from architecture.

Juan O'Gorman prepared his mosaics in slabs, one meter square, and applied them to the superstructure of the library much in the same spirit that the sculptured blocks of limestone were used to form continuous ornament in the Maya temples. By permitting the movement of his narrative to flow freely over the face of the walls, breaking through its grid form, he arrives at a kind of history writing which takes into account the movement of the observer.

"In working out the composition for the four walls of the library," he says, "the first thing was to find a scale of plastic values to fit the building, one which would be correct in size when seen from various points of view, without

153

154

155

Here is shown the process of expanding the cartoon (#153) to modular units.

over-small detail or over-large figures, which would have destroyed the monumentality of the building. The second thing was to relate the material of each wall to the composition of the four walls so that they would count as one unit plastically and esthetically. In the third place, it was necessary to bring each of the four walls into dynamic symmetry so the total composition would form one geometric structure in three dimensions, while its time dimension was given in the historical theme depicting a different period of Mexico's culture for each wall."

Drawings for the library walls were first made in small scale, then copied in reverse in full scale on heavy paper marked off into square meters. The cartoon was then cut up and laid on the ground where moulds, also one meter square, were placed over each unit. The stones were then laid on the drawing and the mold filled with an inch of concrete. Steel reinforcing rods with anchor hooks were sunk into the concrete so that the slabs could be attached to a trellis of steel already fixed to the library walls. When the concrete had cured, the paper was stripped away and the stones wire-brushed. Joints between the 4,000 separate slabs were filled with additional concrete after they had been hooked into place.

O'Gorman first tried out natural stone mosaics in his own house in San Angel and later, in his house in the Pedregal. In both houses he

156

Juan O'Gorman and one of his mosaics at his home in the Pedregal.

applied the stone directly to a mastic spread on the surface of the walls, floor, or ceiling. It is not by accident, O'Gorman thinks, that mosaics have played a large role in the architecture of fantasy. "Antonio Gaudi used ceramic mosaics as a necessary complement to the baroque forms of his great architecture, and it is evident that without the mosaics he could never have achieved the wonderful snake-like balustrade in the Guell Park at Barcelona, Spain, (#159) nor the color and texture of the roofs, walls, and pinnacles of his great buildings."

In speaking of his admiration for Fernand Cheval's magic palace of Hauterives, France, and Raymond Isidor's poetic Chateau des Assiettes Cassees (Castle of Broken Plates), in Chartres, O'Gorman says, "These breaths of freshness and pure creation, where the imagination is applied for the expression of freedom, are a wonderful relief in the stagnant academic atmosphere of our pretentious commercial modern times, and reveal the aspiration of liberty of the common people, their love of decorative free expression, which is the beneficial character of the baroque. I use the word baroque because I cannot find a better one to designate the complicated, colorful, and intricate possibilities of an architecture using mosaics, whether on the flat or curved surfaces of walls and ceilings, or as a permanent form to polychrome sculpture.

"The advantage of mosaic over painting is the greater consistency achieved in architecture, because they are built into the architecture. Another advantage is the possibility of their use on the outside of buildings, and this brings us into the realm of color as part of architecture, which in antiquity and up to the Renaissance was always an essential part of the composition."

157

158

159

GLOSSARY OF TERMS

ANTICO — Ancient.
BOND — Type of overlapping of tesserae as in laying brick.
BULL-NOSE — Quarter-round tessera used for making corners.
BUTTERING — Spreading mortar on each tessera before laying into setting bed.
BYZANTINE — Historical period preceding Renaissance.
COSMATI — Roman marble cutters of 12th century who did intarsia work; named after two brothers who revived the ancient art.
ENAMELS — Older term applied to highest quality hand-made opaque vitreous composition sometimes called smalti or glass-mosaic.
GROUT — Rich mortar made very thin with water to fill joints between tesserae in a completed installation.
HEADER — A tessera laid with end exposed in face of completed mosaic.
INTAGLIO — Cut into, or depress below surface, as in creating images in relief; sometimes used in conjunction with mosaic.
INTARSIA — Marble, cut and inlaid in mosaic-technique.
MINERAL OXIDES — Colors used to tint the grout; also used to create color in smalti or enamels.
MURIATIC ACID — Commercial term for hydrochloric acid

ORO — Italian term for gold; often used to describe gold leaf tesserae where the gold has been flashed on.
POLYCHROME — Many colored.
ROUT — To cut out a channel in marble, wood, etc.
SMALTI — Italian term for highest quality of hand-made glass, mosaic or enamels, often called Byzantine glass.
TESSERA — Small piece of marble, glass, stone, etc., having square or nearly square face used in mosaic work; to tesselate means to arrange the tesserae (plural).
TOOTHING — Technique of seaming prefabricated sections of mosaic to conceal joints by lapping over every other row of tessera.
VITREOUS — Like glass or derived from glass.

Note: Latin terms are also used to categorize older types of mosaic work: *Opus Sectile*, inlaying of larger stones or pieces of marble for flooring, as revived by the Cosmati brothers in 12th century Rome; *Opus Tesselatum*, patterns of geometric shapes done in cubes of marble; and *Opus Vermiculatum*, meaning small stones of tesserae arranged in curved lines, sometimes forming actual pictures.

SELECTED BIBLIOGRAPHY

BOOKS
A HISTORY OF MOSAICS
by E. W. Anthony, Porter Sargent, Boston, 1935
ART IN EUROPEAN ARCHITECTURE
by Paul Damaz, Reinhold, New York, 1956
ART IN MODERN ARCHITECTURE
by Eleanor Bittermann, Reinhold, New York, 1952
BYZANTINE PAINTING
by Andre Graber, Skira, New York, 1953
ROMAN PAINTING
by Amadeo Maiuri, Skira, New York, 1953
RAVENNA MOSAICS
by Giuseppe Bovini, New York Graphic Society, New York, 1956

PERIODICALS
ART AND CRAFT OF MAKING MOSAICS
by M. Lyon, House Beautiful, August 1955
HOW TO MAKE PEBBLE MOSAICS
by H. Bruton, House Beautiful, July 1954
HOW TO MAKE PEBBLED MOSAICS FOR GARDEN PATHS AND PATIOS
by M. Rudd, House & Garden, May 1953
INTEGRATION OF THE ARTS IN ARCHITECTURE
by Joseph L. Young, Pacific Architect & Builder, May 1956
JEANNE REYNAL'S MOSAICS
by Dore Ashton, Crafts Horizons, December 1956

JOSEPH L. YOUNG CREATES A UNIQUE MOSAIC MURAL
by E. K. Sewell, American Artist, September 1955
JUAN O'GORMAN'S MOSAIC MURAL
by James Norman, American Artist, June 1953
MAKING MODERN CERAMIC MOSAICS
by A. W. Clark, School Arts, May 1956
MOSAIC ART FOR TODAY
by Larry Argiro, School Arts, June 1955
MOSAIC DETAILS FROM A HOUSE BY JUAN O'GORMAN
Arts & Architecture, March 1955
MOSAICS: NEW HOBBY FROM AN ANCIENT ART
Living for Young Homemakers, July 1955
MOSAICS FROM BITS OF COLORED TILE
Ceramics Monthly, January 1955
MOSAICS IN TRANSLUCENT PLASTIC
Sunset, March 1956
ON THE ART CONTROVERSY
by Sister Magdalen Mary, I.H.M., School Arts, November 1956
PROUD BYZANTIUM'S CHRISTIAN TREASURE
Mosaics in the Churches of Istanbul, Life, December 1950
REVIVAL IN MOSAICS
House & Garden, December 1956
ROMAN LIFE IN 1600 YEAR OLD COLOR PICTURES
by G. V. Centili, National Geographic, February 1957
SAHL SWARZ MAKES A NEW APPROACH TO AN ANCIENT ART
American Artist, June 1955
TILES AND MOSAICS IN ADVERTISING
by P. K. Brooks, American Artist, June 1955

The techniques shown on pages 34-37 are from the 16mm color film, THE WORLD OF MOSAIC, produced in cooperation with the University of California, Los Angeles and available from many film libraries.

524

CREDITS

Jacket design by Jerrold Simon

PHOTOS:

Brick Manufacturers Association, The, 17
Fiorenza, Vito, (back end paper)
Flax, M., Art Supplies, 85
French Government Tourist Office, 19
Healey, Dale, 29-36
Immaculate Heart College, 57-59, 61
Italian State Tourist Office, 4, 11, 26
Jacobs, Lou, Jr., 98

Jones, A. Quincy, AIA, 6
Korsakaite, Ada, 2
Kraushaar Galleries, 79
Lang, Erwin, 158
Los Angeles Chamber of Commerce, 10, 18
Los Angeles Tile Jobbers, 39
Malcolm, Bonnie Jean, 60
Manufacturers Trust of New York, 9
McCoy, Esther, 152-56, 158
Mosaic Tile Company, 2, 15-16, 148
New York Times Studio, 72
Inc., 133

Schaefer, Bertha, Gallery, 72
Shore, David, 7, 20-21, 23, 25, 90-97, 99-104, 106, 110, 141
Shulman, Julius, 1, 78, 80, 89
Southern California, Universit
Stanford University, 14
Stewart, Albert, 17
Tolbert, Mildred, 112, 115
Tile Council of America, 71, 78
Tile Magazine, 138
Wisconsin, University of, 136
World of Mosaic, The, 12-13
Young, Leslie Sybil, 5, 22, 38,
oung, Cecily, 107-09, 130,